ANIMALS ON THE EDGE

Elephants UNDER PRESSURE

A Cause and Effect Investigation

by Kathy Allen

Consultant:
Gay Bradshaw, PhD
Author of *Elephants on the Edge: What Animals Teach Us about Humanity*
Director of the Kerulos Center
Jacksonville, Oregon

CAPSTONE PRESS
a capstone imprint

Fact Finders are published by Capstone Press,
151 Good Counsel Drive, P.O. Box 669, Mankato, Minnesota 56002.
www.capstonepub.com

Library of Congress Cataloging-in-Publication Data
Allen, Kathy.
  Elephants under pressure : a cause and effect investigation / by Kathy Allen.
    p. cm. — (Fact finders. Animals on the edge)
  Summary: "Describes the cause and effect of elephant and human encounters"—Provided
by publisher.
  ISBN 978-1-4296-4534-8 (library binding)
  1. Elephants—Effect of human beings on—Juvenile literature. 2. Elephants—Behavior—Juvenile
literature. I. Title. II. Series.

QL737.P98.A46 2011
599.67'15—dc22

2010008562

Editorial Credits
Mari Bolte, editor; Ashlee Suker, designer; Kelly Garvin, media researcher;
    Eric Manske, production specialist

Photo Credits
Alamy/Ian Wood, 7 (middle right); Whitehead Images, 22
AP Images/Victoria Kuehne, 5
CORBIS/Stephen Morrison/epa, 21; Ted Wood/Aurora Photos, 14
Dreamstime/Johnshamandjp, 7 (bottom right); Leksele, 7 (middle left); Mhpiper, 23;
    Pniesen, cover; Robert Hardholt, 7 (top left); Shariff Che' Lah, 7 (bottom left)
Getty Images/AFP, 18; Mitch Kezar, 27; Thomas Backer, 16; Tom Stoddart Archive, 13
Newscom/Emmanuel Dunand, 11
Peter Arnold/P. Weimann, 7 (top right)
Photoshot Holdings/David Higgs, 26; Mike Lane, 12
Shutterstock/Andreas Nilsson, 25; Peter Betts, 8; polispoliviou, design elements (elephant skin);
    Steve Noakes, 15
Visuals Unlimited/Adam Jones, 4

TABLE OF CONTENTS

CHAPTER 1

When Elephants Act Up

Throughout history elephants have performed many roles for humans. In India they are worshipped and are led through city streets in colorful costumes for festivals. In Southeast Asia, elephants work, carrying heavy loads for humans. Baby elephants have been used to greet hotel guests in Thailand. There, tourists pay to feed and pet elephants on the street.

Elephants have lived and worked near people in places like Thailand for thousands of years.

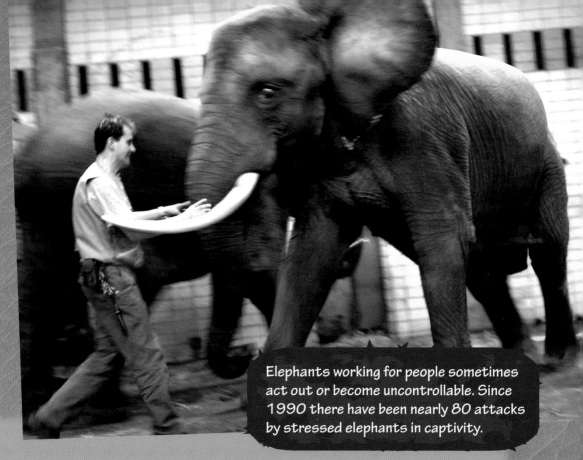

Elephants working for people sometimes act out or become uncontrollable. Since 1990 there have been nearly 80 attacks by stressed elephants in captivity.

But recently elephants have done new and terrifying things. A stampeding elephant in southern Thailand trampled three plantation workers. Another crushed two women in Indonesia. In India, seven people died when an elephant was separated from its herd and panicked. Elephants block traffic in Africa. They roam towns and villages in Asia. And 500 people around the world are killed by wild and captive elephants every year.

One thing is clear. Elephants and people are not getting along—and sometimes the results are deadly.

Humans have long had contact with elephants. Early humans hunted the mammoth, a relative of the elephant. Most human cultures lived in relative peace with their elephant neighbors. Around the world elephants are viewed with awe and wonder. So what could be causing the sudden clash between humans and elephants? Why is the usually peaceful elephant beginning to act aggressively? To understand why elephants are acting out, you need to look at how their lives have changed.

Elephants are big, strong animals. They can grow to be 13 feet (4 meters) tall and weigh 15,000 pounds (6,804 kilograms). In many places elephants are used as beasts of burden. Typically they are taken from their mothers at a very young age. Life in **captivity** is hard and very different from the way they would live in the wild. Some elephants are beaten and abused by their owners. Even if they are treated well, elephants living near people can be under severe stress.

captivity—the condition of being kept or held by force

Kinds of Elephants

Savanna

Forest

Indian

Sumatran

Sri Lankan

Borneo

Both humans and elephants are social creatures. Like humans, groups of elephants live and work together. And both elephants and humans learn from older **society** members. Young elephants live in large groups with older females called allomothers.

Female elephants without their own calves fill the role of allomother.

Older elephants care for calves and teach them how to behave. Calves also learn how to find water and food. As they get older, young females stay with the group to teach the next generation. Male elephants, called bulls, leave the herd when they are about 10 years old. They will find a group of other males. The older bulls teach the younger ones how to behave around other elephants.

Elephants are like people in other ways. Elephants have large, complex brains. Their brains allow them to have societies, emotions, and intelligence. They can also use tools and have a complicated communication system. Lifelong relationships exist between herd members.

Traditionally, elephant societies were made up of thousands of family groups across Asia and Africa. These interconnected groups were part of a large web of relationships. Family members communicated and maintained their relationships with each other by **migrating** across the continents. But in recent years this elephant society has begun to break down.

society—a group of elephants who live in the same area

migrate—to move from one place to another

WHAT IS HAPPENING TO ELEPHANT SOCIETY?

CHAPTER 2
All in the Family

Every year the number of people living in Africa and Asia increases. As human populations grow, so do their need for land and resources. People build homes and farm land where elephants once lived. Elephants seeking food and water are forced to look elsewhere. Homes and gardens stand in the middle of their age-old paths. Their forests and grasslands are now farms and plantations.

With farmland dotting the landscape, elephants cannot travel freely. They can no longer move from place to place. Without the ability to migrate across the continent, they are cut off from the main elephant society.

Sharing land puts humans and elephants in closer contact every day. For some elephant populations, this contact means trouble. Wild elephants have been seen with wounds from bullets and other weapons. Some have lost their tusks after becoming tangled in traps.

The city of Bangkok, Thailand, banned elephants from being brought into the city in 2000. This law has not stopped the practice.

But the story gets worse. Herds of elephants are disappearing. Scientists estimate that as many as 100,000 Asian elephants roamed in the wild in the early 1900s. Today there may be as few as 38,000. Most of these elephants live in India. Although India is only one-third the size of the United States, more than three times as many people live there.

People and elephants live closer together than ever before.

Humans crowd out elephants in African countries as well. In 1979 there were 1.2 million wild African elephants. This number dropped to 60,000 in only 10 years. Many of these elephants were killed by **poachers**. Elephants are hunted by poachers for their meat, hides, and ivory tusks.

Ivory is carved to make everything from jewelry to small statues to stamps. In the 1980s, countries around the world banned the ivory trade. Leaders hoped that the killing of elephants would stop.

Since the ban, selling ivory has gone underground. Elephants are still in danger. Poachers kill more than 38,000 African elephants every year.

poacher—a person who hunts certain animals even though it is against the law

Elephant tusks can cost as much as $1,000 each.

Shorter Lives, Smaller Tusks

Elephant tusks today are smaller than they were 100 years ago. Back then, elephants were not hunted as much. They lived longer and were able to grow tusks that weighed more than 200 pounds (91 kg). Today tusks weighing 30 pounds (14 kg) are considered large. In some areas, elephants no longer have tusks.

Some scientists believe poaching reduces the number of elephants with tusks. Others say that this is an **adaptation**. They think that elephants with smaller tusks would be less visible to poachers. Over time, more elephants are born without the ability to grow tusks.

adaptation—a change a living thing goes through to better fit in with its environment

People are forcing elephants to destroy their own habitat.

Humans are also destroying the forests where elephants live. Some countries have banned logging in those forests. But logging still happens in much of Asia. On the island of Sumatra, more than half the forests have been destroyed since the 1980s. In 2005 alone, 11 percent of the island's forest was lost. In Thailand, elephants are forced to destroy their own homes. They are used to drag or carry wood out of the forest.

Loss of forests has crowded elephants into smaller and smaller areas. In some countries, parks for elephants have been created. It is hoped that elephants will be able to live safely away from humans.

Losing their homes and families causes elephants to lash out at people and other elephants.

But parks are too small to support so many large animals. For centuries wild elephant herds lived peacefully. Now they are chased away from their homes and forced to live in crowded areas. Families are separated and young elephants are left without parents.

Many bull elephants may act aggressively toward other male elephants after suffering such trauma. Fights can lead to severe wounds or even death. Elephants are dying from too little land to live on.

HOW DOES HABITAT LOSS AFFECT ELEPHANTS?

CHAPTER 3

Staying Alive

Elephants eat many of the same foods humans eat. But they need a lot more of it. An African elephant can wash down 600 pounds (272 kg) of food and another 60 gallons (227 liters) of water every day. In India elephants spend two-thirds of the day eating. They eat corn, bananas, sugar cane, and other vegetables that farmers grow.

Some elephants are forced to eat garbage to survive. They sometimes eat broken bottles, plastic bags, and other harmful waste.

In Asia, between 10,000 and 15,000 elephants work for people. It's a big job to keep all these animals fed. While some elephants are treated well, others are starved so they will obey. Others have owners who aren't able to provide the huge amounts of food their elephants need to stay healthy. A hungry elephant is much more likely to rebel against its keeper.

Farmers in Asia and Africa are in a constant battle to keep elephants away from their crops. Just one or two elephants can destroy an entire season's worth of crops. Some farms are near areas set aside as elephant **sanctuaries**. For elephants living nearby, crops are an easy source of food in safe areas. And elephants are not afraid of the farmers because they see them all the time. Some brave elephants may even enter houses. They raid kitchens and pantries for food.

sanctuary—a natural area where animals are protected

Building damage is often caused by elephants searching for food and water.

Elephants need more than just food. They also need space. They may roam over an area of 850 square miles (2,200 square kilometers) as they travel to watering holes. Elephant leaders have gained detailed knowledge over years of life experience. They use this knowledge to find food and water. They also know safe places for the herd to go during periods when food and water is limited. To find food and water, elephants need to be able to travel freely.

But elephants are no longer able to use their wealth of knowledge. When an entire generation of elephants dies, the wisdom held by older elephants is lost. The herd will no longer know how to safely find food. Instead, they might lead their herdmates to easy food sources like farms.

Human farmlands dot elephants' migration routes. When elephants raid a crop, they are likely to meet the farmer who planted it. These meetings often become elephant attacks.

Many farmers try to frighten the elephants away. But a farmer banging pots and pans or shooting a gun in the air may make the problem worse. Already under stress, a spooked elephant is even more at risk of panicking. People or objects in the way might be trampled. An elephant feeling cornered could lash out and hurt or kill someone. When elephants kill humans, it gives people false ideas of what they are like.

Gentle elephants are under huge stress. They are constantly threatened by humans. Elephants fear anything that may kill or hurt them. So it is not surprising when they try to protect themselves and their families. More elephant attacks are being reported worldwide. In fact, the conflict between elephants and people is called the H.E.C., or Human-Elephant Conflict.

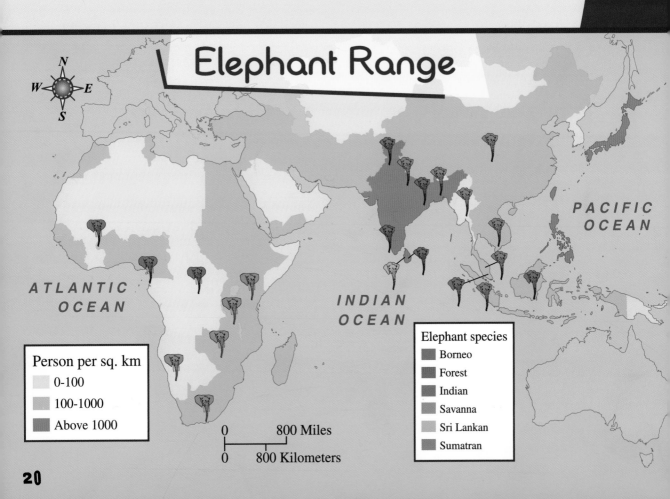

Elephant Range

N W E S

PACIFIC OCEAN

ATLANTIC OCEAN

INDIAN OCEAN

Person per sq. km
- 0-100
- 100-1000
- Above 1000

Elephant species
- Borneo
- Forest
- Indian
- Savanna
- Sri Lankan
- Sumatran

0 — 800 Miles

0 — 800 Kilometers

Elephant calves are often left without parents due to poachers. Some elephant experts care for these calves until they are old enough to go back to wild herds.

Researchers now know that many elephant attacks come from herds that have been poached. Like humans, elephants care for the sick and mourn for the dead. Seeing family killed by hunters is not something an elephant can easily forget.

Some herds have members old enough to recall times when humans were friends. But when those members die, the knowledge is lost. The new generation of elephants is raised knowing only conflict with humans.

WHY SHOULD YOU CARE ABOUT KEEPING ELEPHANTS SAFE?

CHAPTER 4

Becoming Friends Again

Elephants can cause thousands of dollars worth of crop and garden damage.

Conflicts between humans and elephants hurt both species. When elephants raid crops, farmers are upset about their lost money. They begin to view elephants as pests. If they see elephants attack, they may start to fear the huge animals.

One study found that Forest elephants spread as many as 55 different species of plant seeds.

In reality elephants are not pets, pests, or killers. They are part of nature and have been for millions of years. And Earth is their home too.

What elephants do and how they live helps other animals, trees, and plants to thrive. Elephants spread seeds of the plants they eat. When elephants walk through forests, they create new paths and expose plants to fresh air and sunlight. Many animals and plants could not live where they do if it weren't for elephants.

Wildlife groups and scientists teach the public about the importance of elephants. They want people to understand the many similarities between humans and elephants.

Conservation scientists teach farmers to see elephants as neighbors, not threats. They hope to create unity between elephants and farmers. In many countries, more money can be made from tourists coming to see elephants than from poaching. Tourism and teaching often spark a love for elephants. This love leads to the protection of elephant habitats too. This protection helps countless other plants and animals.

Others try to educate people about captive elephants. Elephants do not live long in zoos. In the wild, they can live into their 40s or 50s. Zoo elephants are lucky if they reach age 20.

Zoo elephants are also more likely to suffer from health-related issues. Many experience weight gain, illness, or mental stress. Stressed or unhappy mother elephants in zoos may injure or kill their babies.

Some zoos have stopped displaying elephants altogether. They believe that elephants are better off in sanctuaries or in the wild.

People can learn to live peacefully with elephants like they have in the past.

People have tried to keep elephants at a distance. Some farmers dig trenches or put fences around their fields. A new trick is to use chili bombs. These dry bombs burst out a dust of strong, spicy chilies. The elephants hate the chilies and stay away. In India, groups of tame elephants and people lead wild elephants back to the forest.

These measures may help stop conflict between elephants and humans for a short while. But the real solution is for people to learn how to live peacefully with elephants. Humans and elephants have lived as neighbors. People need to remember that coexisting with wildlife is always a possibility.

People try to move elephants to safe areas. But moving elephants is expensive and doesn't always work.

Elephants play a large role in their environment and people's lives.

People have the responsibility to learn to live peacefully with elephants. Reading and learning about elephants is one way to help. The more you know about elephants, the more you can do to keep these amazing creatures safe.

Elephant Society

Elephant society
(can include hundreds or
thousands of elephants)

↓

Elephant clan
(around 70 elephants)

↓

Family unit
(eight to 15 related elephants)
Led by a female who leads
the herd until she dies. Her
eldest female offspring will
be the next leader

Male elephants reach
maturity around age 10.
They leave the family unit
and join an all-male herd.

Female elephants reach
maturity around age 11 or 12
They stay in the same herd
their whole lives.

After mating, the
female is pregnant
for 22–24 months.

↓

Baby elephant depends on its
mother for four to five years.

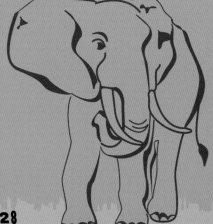

RESOURCES TO HELP ELEPHANTS

THE DAVID SHELDRICK WILDLIFE TRUST

The David Sheldrick Wildlife Trust works closely with Tsavo National Park, Kenya's largest wildlife refuge. The Wildlife Trust helps raise and heal the park's orphaned elephants and rhinos. Since its founding in 1977, the Wildlife Trust has raised more than 80 African elephants.

THE ELEPHANT SANCTUARY IN TENNESSEE

The largest natural-habitat refuge for elephants in the United States, the Elephant Sanctuary provides care to both African and Asian elephants. This nonprofit group cares for sick or needy elephants on more than 2,700 acres (1,090 hectares) of land.

THE KERULOS CENTER

The Kerulos Center is a nonprofit group that helps animals recover from trauma. The Center seeks to create a partnership between animals and humans. The group works to help people recognize the role animals play in peoples' lives.

SAVE THE ELEPHANTS

Save the Elephants encourages studies on elephant behaviors. The group uses GPS tracking systems to learn more about how elephants live. Members also use this tracking system to follow ivory traders and poachers. Their goal is to help people learn how to live with elephants as neighbors, not as threats.

Glossary

adaptation (a-dap-TAY-shuhn)—a change a living thing goes through to better fit in with its environment

captivity (kap-TIV-ih-tee)—the condition of being kept or held by force

habitat (HAB-uh-tat)—the natural place and conditions in which a plant or animal lives

ivory (EYE-vur-ee)—the natural substance from which the tusks and teeth of some animals are made

migrate (MYE-grate)— to move from one place to another when seasons change or when food is scarce

poacher (POHCH-ur)—a person who hunts or fishes illegally

sanctuary (SANGK-choo-er-ee)—a natural area where plants and animals are protected from harm

society (suh-SYE-uh-tee)—a group of elephants who live in the same area

stress (STRESS)—strain or pressure

tusk (TUSK)—one of a pair of long, pointed teeth of a woolly mammoth, an elephant, or a walrus

Read More

Firestone, Mary. *Top 50 Reasons to Care about Elephants: Animals in Peril*. Top 50 Reasons to Care about Endangered Animals. Berkeley Heights, N.J.: Enslow Publishers, 2010.

Hirschmann, Kris. *Elephants*. Animals Attack. Detroit: KidHaven Press, 2006.

Turner, Matt. *Asian Elephant*. Animals under Threat. Chicago: Heinemann Library, 2005.

Internet Sites

FactHound offers a safe, fun way to find Internet sites related to this book. All of the sites on FactHound have been researched by our staff.

Here's all you do:

Visit *www.facthound.com*

FactHound will fetch the best sites for you!

Index

FRIENDS FREE LIBRARY
GERMANTOWN FRIENDS LIBRARY
5418 Germantown Avenue
Philadelphia, PA 19144
215-951-2355

Each borrower is responsible for all items
checked out on his/her library card, for
fines on materials kept overtime, and
replacing any lost or damaged materials.